Eros Paradise

AF176637

Sex -
a fountain of youth and
health

Printed and published by:
BoD - Books on Demand, Norderstedt
ISBN 9783754308370
Cover picture: Fountain in Paris
Photo: Eros Paradise

Table of contents

First letter

Dear Mr. Paradise,

I have expressed to your publisher the wish to correspond with you. Afterwards I did not receive your name but at least your PO box address.

Basically everything started with one of your romantic love stories. As I lived alone since the death of my husband, your love story touched my heart and gave me the idea to look for a partner again. Therefore I published the following newspaper advertisement in December:

'Attractive, single lady seeks single gentleman for walks together and to attend the Christmas concert at the opera.'

Since I had concealed my advanced age, I received numerous letters. As a passionate violinist, I replied to a former piano teacher. For half a year now, my new partner has accompanied me daily on walks along the banks of the Rhine and playing the violin on the piano.

We celebrated the 90th birthday of my partner four weeks ago in a luxury hotel high obove the Rhine. In the same hotel we celebrated my 90th birthday yesterday. My partner played the piano piece 'Invitation to dance' by Carl Maria von Weber. Afterwards he asked me to dance the opening waltz with him. As a birthday present he gave me a red parcel and with a wink asked me to open it at home. After removing the wrapping paper, I couldn't believe my eyes: In front of me was a bright red sexy underwear set with a push-up bra. At that moment I understood: with my piano player the music is still playing somewhere else.

At the same time, I remembered an article about the man's strong sex drive, in which it was reported that the actor Charlie Chaplin had fathered a child at the age of 73, the actor Antony Quinn at 81. The Guinness world record holder, a man in Australia, even succeeded on this at the age of 93 years.

As I could live quite well without sex as a widow until now, I sat in front of the red push-up bra in complete shok. Suddenly I had an idea:

Maybe my partner had not bought the right cup size. Then I wouldn't have to wear the sexy underwear at all and could return the suggestive gift with my best thanks. After I had put on the

6

push-up bra, I looked at myself in the mirror. What bad luck! The bra fit perfectly.

Why I am telling you, a complete stranger, a story about the perfect size of my push-up bra when I've been reluctant to talk to my husband about intimate matters for 40 years? The comments interspersed in your stories reveal a considerable amount of medical expertise. That's why I'm sure that your pseudonym Eros Paradise stands for a doctor.

The push-up bra, which I can only understand as an 'invitation to have sex', confronts me with a strong pressure to make a decision. Therefore I need your medical advice:

My father died of a heart attack at the age of 105 years. My family doctor informed me about the main causes of the heart attack: high blood sugar, high cholesterol and high blood pressure. My blood sugar and cholesterol levels are normal. However, I have high blood pressure. Unfortunately, I do not tolerate all antihypertensive tablets very well.

Are you aware of a study that shows that regular sexual activity increases the risk of heart attack or blood pressure in women? I can only hope that you answer one of these questions or preferably both in the affirmative in your reply letter. Then I would have a good medical reason, not to wear the perfectly fitting push-up bra and could continue to limit myself to walking, making music and dancing with my partner.

Please send your answer to the PO box address on the envelope. As the publisher was not willing to tell me your name, I will sign my letter with an alias only for reasons of discretion.

Yours sincerely

Eve

Second letter

Dear Miss Eve,

thank you very much for your letter of 2 June.

In 2019, the University of Michigan conducted a study of 2204 men and women between the ages of 57 and 85. The study group consisted of a sexually active group and an equal-size abstinent group. The study examined how often the men and women in the two groups suffered a heart attack within a period of five years.

Men who had sexual intercourse at least once a week were twice as likely to have a heart attack as senior citizens without sex. In contrast, older women can reduce the risk of heart attack through sex. According to a study in the journal 'Biological Psychology', sex can also lower blood pressure in older women.

An often quoted saying by Martin Luther is:

'Twice in a week does no harm to him or her, making a hundred and four in the year.'

According to the Michigan study, the claimed harmlessness of having sex *twice a week is true for older women, but not for men in this age group.*

Since you were shoked by the 'invitation to have sex', the Michigan study at least gives you the opportunity to convince your partner of the necessity of a moderate frequency of sexual intercourse by pointing out his increased risk of heart attack, and thus somewhat reduce the pressure to make a decision triggered by your perfectly fitting push-up bra.

However, the Michigan study puts you in a difficult position: On the one hand, you probably want to reduce your partner's risk of heart attack as much as possible by keeping the frequency of sexual intercourse at a low level. On the other hand, you have the opportunity to lower your blood pressure by having frequent orgasms and then stop taking the antihypertensive tablets, which you all tolerate poorly.

I regret that in your case I cannot deduce from the Michigan study any 'good medical reason' against sexual activity that you were hoping for.

Yours sincerely

Eros Paradise

Third letter

Dear Mr. Paradise,

thank you for the prompt reply to my letter of 2 June.

You recommend that we keep the frequency of sexual intercourse 'at a low level'. This will certainly be difficult for my lover, but not at all for me. As I am writing this letter under the protection of anonymity, I now confess a fact that my husband has never heard of me in 40 years of marriage:

During intercourse I felt a slight sexual arousal, but I never achieved orgasm, which I always played to my husband by moaning loudly, as it flattered his vanity to be able to bring me to the climax. I was very disappointed, of course, never to get an orgasm, while he always experienced the climax after a very short time.

Since frequent orgasms in older women lower blood pressure, you recommend that I have regular orgasms. Can a woman who has never experienced a climax during sexual intercourse reach orgasm through masturbation?

You will be surprised to learn from me

11

that despite my advanced age, I cannot answer this question based on my own experience. Because of my strictly religious boarding school education masturbation had the stigma of a serious sin for me. Therefore I never tried to achieve orgasm this way.

In my case, however, you have claimed a medical reason for having orgasms on a regular basis. If I can reach orgasm through masturbation, although I never reached the climax during marital intercourse, I would ask you to answer the following question:

What is the safest and fastest masturbation method to achieve orgasm? In order to be able to recognize this at all, I should know about the characteristic features of an orgasm. Since I have never had an orgasm in my life, I would like to ask you to inform me about the most important characteristics of female orgasm and to answer this letter as soon as possible.

Yours sincerely

Eve

Fourth letter

Dear Miss Eve,

thank you for your letter of 7 June.
I do not know your name. You do not know my name either, because my 48 books have been published in several languages under different pseudonyms. This anonymity makes it easier for me to answer your questions, which touch the intimate area.
I can imagine how frustrating it was for you to have to fake a non-existent orgasm for 40 years by moaning loudly. But you share this fate with many women. This is proven by a surwey of 1417 women.
When asked 'Do you achieve orgasm during sexual intercourse?' the following answers were ticked off: always: 11 %, often: 17 %, in half of the cases: 17 %, rarely: 29 % and never: 26 %.
A quarter of the women are therefore in the same situation as you.
Because of your strictly boarding school education you never tried to masturbate. Fortunately, in our enlightened society the attitude towards masturbation has changed.
Most men and women today

experience masturbation as a normal form of sexuality and have done so since their youth.

A recent survey found that about half of all 15-year old girls have already given themselves an orgasm by hand. The masturbation can also improve sex between two people. A woman who discovers during masturbation what gives her particular pleasure can request this from her partner and thus reach orgasm more often.

The question of whether a woman who has never experienced orgasm during sexual intercourse can reach orgasm through masturbation can be clearly answered in the affirmative on the basis of modern sexual research.

The father of psychoanalysis, Sigmund Freud, advocated the thesis that only when a penis enters the vagina can the woman experience a strong orgasm (vaginal orgasm). This thesis has been disproved by modern sexual research. Only a small percentage of women can achieve orgasm simply by movements of the 'magic wand' so highly regarded by Sigmund Freud. In most cases an additional stimulation of the clitoris is necessary, which can be achieved by appropriate body movements of the partners.

Women who do not experience an

orgasm during intercourse can never-
theless achieve orgasm by stimulating
their clitoris (clitoral orgasm). Many
women find the clitoral orgasm trig-
gerred by masturbation much more
pleasurable than the vaginal orgasm
triggered by movements of the penis.
This is perhaps an explanation for the
surprising result of an American study
conducted in 2007:

Masturbation is about as frequent in
women who live in a partnership as in
women living alone.

Contrary to Sigmund Freud's thesis,
there are even women who already
achieve a strong orgasm through sex-
ual fantasies.

You ask which is the safest and fastest
way to achieve orgasm. For anatomi-
cal reasons I recommend rubbing the
clitoris. This sexual organ is not just a
little 'pearl of orgasm' that you can
feel in the vagina. The strength of the
clitoral orgasm is based on the fact
that the clitoris extends 10 cm into the
vagina.

During masturbation, the rise in the
female arousal curve is steeper than
the rise in the male arousal curve, be-
cause 800 nerves end in the 'pearl of
orgasm' but only 400 in the man's
'magic wand'.

Most women do not have any

15

problems with orgasm when they are rubbing their 'pearl of orgasm'. Clitoral stimulation is therefore the safest and fastest way to achieve strong sexual arousal and the peak of orgasm.

You ask me about the characteristic features by which you can recognize an orgasm. I will answer this question within the framework of the four phase model of the sex researchers William Masters and Virginia Johnson.

1. The arousal phase
As your blood vessels dilate, more blood flows to the external sex organs. The labia, vagina and clitoris swell. Your vagina gets wet. Your breasts swell. Your nipples are erect. Your breathing will be faster.

2. The plateau phase
Your pulse is getting faster. Blood pressure is rising. The tension in your pelvic muscles is increasing. The sexual arousal has now reached a certain level (plateau) and is increasing only slowly.

3. The orgasm
The endocrine glands secrete the happiness hormon 'dopamine', which arouses the whole body. There are

rhythmic contractions of the uterus and vagina. During ecstatic orgasm up to 15 muscle contractions can occur. Your pulse rate can double.

The average duration of orgasm is up to one minute for women and between 3 and 12 seconds for men.

In contrast to the man, the woman can experience several orgasms one after the other in a short period of time (so called multiple orgasm).

4. The relaxation phase
Your cardiovascular functions are nor- malizing. The vaginal swelling takes about 15 minutes to go down, while the labia may take up to 3 hours.

Hopefully this time I have given you the answers you expected.

Yours sincerely

Eros Paradise

Fifth letter

Dear Mr. Paradise,

while looking for a ruler, I happened to find in my partner's drawer the duplicates of the letters she wrote to you on 2 and 7 June. So I will take the liberty of asking you some questions as well:

For some time now I've been having problems with my erection. The prolonged erection required for sexual intercourse is often absent. Because of these erectile dysfunctions, my partner of many years has separated from me.

What are the possible causes for the occurence of impotence? What are the treatment options?

My partner has not yet thanked me for my birthday present, but reading the letter she wrote to you on 2 June, I learned of her shock at the sight of the red sexy underwear. Therefore I decided to make the following, for me very embarrassing confession to her tomorrow:

Since I have erection problems there is only one way for me to achieve

18

*strong sexual arousal, which then en-
ables the longer lasting erection necessary for sexual intercourse:*

*The sight of a woman dressed in sexy
underwear.*

*However, I only discovered this path
after my former partner had already
left me. For this reason I gave my new
partner who despite her old age still
has fantastic breasts, the red sexy underwear for her 90th birthday.*

*In the evening when I imagined her
standing in front of the mirror with
her push-up bra and looking at her
well-rounded breasts, I immediately
got a turbo-erection.*

*Surprisingly, it is not difficult for me
to confess my perverse inclination to
you, although I have not had the cou-
rage to tell my partner about this inclination in the last two weeks.*

*Hopefully you can explain to me from
a medical point of view why I can only
get sexually aroused by the sight of a
woman dressed in sexy underwear.*

*Unfortunately, reading the letter that
my partner wrote to you on 7th June, I
learned that although she feels a sexual arousal during sexual intercourse,
she never reachs orgasm.*

*I would like to bring her to a strong
arousal and climax by stimulating her
erogenous zones. My former partner*

19

always wanted to have sexual inter-course without much foreplay, as this would cause her to have multiple or-gasms. That is why I have not had the opportunity to explore the erogenous zones of the female body thoroughly. I therefore ask you answer the follo-wing questions:

Where are the erogenous zones of the female body?

Which zones can I use to bring my lo-ved one to a multiple orgasm?

Hopefully, the high blood pressure that my partner mentioned in her let-ter of 2 June does not speak against sexual activity from a medical point of view. Otherwise we would unfortuna-tely have to limit ourselves in future to walks along the banks of the Rhine, making music and dancing.

Since my partner signed both of her letters with an alias, I will also sign this letter with an alias to protect ano-nymity.

Yours sincerely

Adam

Sixth letter

Dear Mr. Adam,

since the two letters from your partner Eve were not only found but also
read by you, I advise you to hide today's letter, which deals with very
intimate   problems of male sexuality,
as well as possible from your partner.

In Cologne from 1998 - 2000 a survey
was conducted among 4489 men aged
30 - 80 years. The following questions
were asked:

Are you sexually active?

Group 30 - 39 years: yes 96 %, group
70-80 years: yes 71 %.

Are you sexually active weekly?

Young group: yes 92 %, old group: yes
41 %.

Do you have problems with erection?
Young group: yes 2 %, old group: yes
53 %.

More than half of the men over 70
years old have poblems with erection.
And yet you are still in a comfortable
position because you get an immediate
'turbo-erection' from the fantasy of a
woman dressed in sexy underwear.

From the information given in your
letter, the diagnosis 'impotence'

cannot be deduced with certainty. Only if a sufficient erection fails to occur in about 70 % of the trials and these problems persist for at least 6 months are the requirements for the diagnosis of impotence fulfilled.

My following explanations are therefore only relevant for you if the presence of impotence is confirmed by a specialist examination.

Impotence is caused in 70 % of cases by physical factors (for example cardiovascular disorders, diabetes mellitus). In the case of arteriosclerosis, not enough blood reaches the penis due to vascular calcification. The amount of blood in the erectile tissue is therefore not sufficient for a stiffening.

In some cases psychological causes are responsable for impotence (for example stress, depression, partnership problems).

According to the Males-study only 58% of impotent men seek medical treatment although diagnostic and therapeutic advances mean that the earlier treatmens begins the better the chances of success.

The ultrasound examination of the blood vessels of the penis is used for diagnostics. In addition the tumescence measurement: With a device you can measure the degree of swelling of the penis during the night. If spontaneous erections are recorded, this prove a functioning erection mechanism. In your case, this mechanism is of course present, as you will immediately get a 'turbo-erection' from the fantasy of a woman dressed in sexy underwear.

For the treatment of impotence you can have your doctor prescribe medication.

The PDE-5 inhibitors fill your erectile tissue with blood, which leads to a stiffening of the penis. The effect of these drugs only begins when you feel sexual arousal.

If tablets are not suitable for you for medical reasons you can inject the active substance into an erectile tissue of the penis.

Alternatively, the active substance can be administered via a plastic applicator inserted into the urethra.

With the vacuum pump you can create a negative pressure that sucks blood into the penis. A rubber ring placed around the root of the penis prevents the blood from draining quickly from the erectile tissue.

You ask me why you only get sexually aroused by the sight of a woman dressed in sexy underwear.

23

If a person can only get sexually aroused through a certain object, the medical term is 'fetishism'. The cause of this sexual deviation has not yet been clarified.

'Fetish' is an inanimate object that the fetishist focuses his interest on. In most cases this is an item of clothing. The fetishist asks his partner to wear a certain item of clothing, for example a red push-up bra during sexual intercourse. You write me how embarrassed you were to confess to your partner the real reason for your unusual birthday present. There is no need for this. Modern sexology does not regard fetishism, which occurs almost exclusively in men, as a perversion but only as a harmless sexual quirk.

With this quirk you are in the best literary society. A classic example of fetishism can already be found in Goethe's 'Faust'. In the first part of the drama, doctor Faust reveals his inclination towards fetishism by asking 'Mephisto' to bring a fetish of 'Gretchen':

Get me something of my sweet angel!
Lead me to her resting place!
Get me a scarf from her breast,
A garter in token of my amorous desire!

Finally, I will answer your question about the erogenous zones of the female body:

The tender stimulation of these sensitive areas takes place during foreplay. In the first phase you should get your partner's feelings going: Tenderly kiss her closed eyelids and mouth. Pamper the outer ear and the earlobe with tongue plays and gentle nibbling. Whisper tender words into her ear. Suck gently on her neck. Do arouse palms and fingertips with a light massage and gentle caressing. Lick and suck on the fingers. Patiently pamper her entire abdominal wall and especially the navel with your nimble tongue. If you stimulate these erogenous zones over a longer period of time, warm waves of lust will flow through your partner's entire body.

In the second phase of foreplay, you should increase this lust by stimulating the most erogenous zones. The lumbar region is one of the most erogenous zones because of the numerous nerves that accompany the spine. By moving your fingers up and down the spine, you will send a pleasent shiver down your partner's lumbar region. By gently massaging the insides of her thighs she will feel a pleasant tingling sensation and anticipation of even more intimate touches. Press lightly with the ball of your hand on her mons veneris and gently caress the swollen labia with your fingertips. If you as an experienced piano player do your finger exercises on these erogenous zones of your loved ones you will elicit the most pleasurable tones from her body's instrument.

However, the ever increasing waves of lust can only carry your loved one to the summit of the climax when the 'orgasm area' in the brain is aroused. Apart from sexual intercourse, there are two best ways to get the woman to climax: Either by stimulating the 'pearl of orgasm' or by arousing the swollen breasts. These two erogenous zones send nerv impulses to the 'orgasm area' of the brain. The stimulation of the 'pearl of orgasm' is done by the fingers or in the so called 'cunnilingus'. This term was formed from the Latin words cunnus / female pubic and lingua / tongue. In this sexual practice, the man arouses the labia, the vaginal vestibule and the 'orgasm pearl' with lips and tongue. It is essential to place a thin latex foil over the vaginal entrance to protect against the transmission of pathogens. The latex foil can be ordered on the

26

internet.

Since according to a survey in Germany only 48 % of women are satisfied by cunnilingus, I don't know if you and your partner are interested in this sexual practice.

Unfortunately, you cannot trigger orgasm by arousing the breasts since your partner always has to wear the push-up bra.

Finally I would like to give you an important advice:

During sexual intercourse the arousal curve of the woman rises much slower than the arousal curve of the man. Therefore you should extend the finger exercices on your partner's erogenous zones for as long as possible. Only then can your partners rising curve of arousal cross the threshold of orgasm. The 'orgasm threshold' is the level of arousal from which an orgasm can be triggered.

Yours sincerely

Eros Paradise

Seventh letter

Dear Mr. Paradise,

yesterday I withdrew my life annuity for the months of May and June in the amount of 20 000 euros from my bank account. When I wanted to hide the money in the piano, I found there the letter which you wrote to my darling on June 20th.

Smiling, I read your advice to hide the letter from me as well as possible. Fortunately, my sweetheart moved from the old people's home to me on june 13th. Otherwise I might never have found your very interisting letter. Due to my strict religious upbringing I know how unseemly it is to read a found letter. But since my darling had gone to so much trouble to find an absolutely safe hiding place for the letter, I could not resist the temptation to do that.

Your remark, that my darling is in a comfortable position with regard to age related erectile dysfuncions, I can only confirm after reading the letter. While other men in his age group for whom treatment of erection problems with tablets is not possible have to *inject a certain medicine into their penis to achieve a strong and long lasting erection, my darling only looks at my pretty push-up bra and its even prettier contents to get a 'turbo-erection' immediately.*

Because of this comfortable position he is also not willing to seek medical treatment for his erection problems. When I said to him:

"My woman's magazine recommended a medical vacuum pump for men with erection problems", he replied:

"There's a much more pleasant way to create a vacuum with me, but I'm ashamed to talk to you about it."

The tips you gave my lover for the first and second phase of the foreplay had a fantastic effect on me. Due to the dexterity of his fingers, which he owes to playing the piano, the long lasting stimulation of my erogenous zones leads each time to a strong sexual arousal. On June 23 I wrote the following text in my diary:

Today I had an orgasm for the first time in my life. In the future, I won't have to fake orgasm by moaning loudly for my lover.

I would like to make love in the dark. But we always have to leave the light on so that my lover can see the push-up bra.

I learned from your letter that there are two best ways to bring a woman to climax apart from sexual intercourse: by stimulatimg the 'pearl of orgasm' or the breasts. I would actually prefer to be brougt to climax by arousing the breasts rather than by stimulating the clitoris. However, this is unfortunately not possible because I always have to wear the push-up bra.

As you pointed out to me about the increased risk of heart attack for my darling in case of frequent sexual intercourse, we limit ourselves to one sexual intercourse per month. However, my lover brings me to clitoral orgasm twice a week by stimulating my erogenous zones.

With my husband the foreplay was always very short, as he reached the climax very quickly. That is why I have never had the opportunity to explore the erogenous zones of the male body thoroughly. Since my lover 'elicits the most pleasurable sounds from my body's instrument' with the stimulation of my erogenous zones recommended by you, I would like to elicit tones of lust from him as well by stimulating the erogenous zones of my darling and thus achieve a 'duet of lust'. Therefore

I ask you to answer the following question:

Where are the most important eroge-nous zones in my darling?

I sincerely hope, thanks to the dexteri-ty of my fingers, which I owe to play-ing the violin, to be as successful as my darling in stimulating the eroge-nous zones. In this case, he might not need the sight of my push-up bra in the future. Then our 'duet of lust' could finally sound in the dark.

Yours sincerely

Eve

Eighth letter

Dear Miss Eve,

in the letter you discovered in the piano, you read a section on the erogenous zones of the woman, which should be stimulated in the first phase of the foreplay. Since these zones are identical in woman and man, I can spare myself the task of enumerating them, and you can limit yourself to repeat your partner's stimulations in the first phase of the foreplay and thus play four-handedly on the 'piano of lust'.

In the second phase of foreplay you should move from the piano of the weakly erogenous zones to the forte of the strongly erogenous zones, all of which are in the genital area. The region between the anus and the scrotum is strongly erogenous. A massage with the fingers directly behind the scrotum will strongly arouse your partner, as this will stimulate the prostate from the outside.

After that you should move on to the pampering program around the glans. This is the male counterpart of the female 'pearl of orgasm'. Because of her thin skin she is very sensitive. The edge of the glans (transition between glans and penis shaft) is particulary erogenous. The frenulum band, which connects the glans with the penis shaft, forms together with the glans the most erogenous zone and is therefore suitable as the maintheme for your 'sonata of lust'. The theme is performed in two variations: Massage with the thumb and stimulation with the tongue.

For the coda of your 'sonata of lust' only one of your darling´s zones is possible: his 'magic wand'. When you arouse this zone, you should start with a tender Adagio of lust and gradually increase it through the Allegro of ecstasy to the Presto of orgasm.

Your partner's reference to a sexual practice he did not want to talk to you about referred to oral sex. In this sexual practice, the woman takes the ‹magic wand› in her mouth and stimulates it with lips and tongue and by blowing. Sucking on the penis is called 'fellatio' (derived from the Latin word fellare / to suck). In a similar way to the medical vacuum pump recommended in your women's magazine, sucking creates a negative pressure that draws blood into the penis, thereby strengthening the erection.

In fellatio and tongue pampering the glans, the transmission of pathogens should be prevented by the use of a condom. Condoms with differents flavours are available for this purpose.

Since, according to a survey in Germany, only 56 percent of men are satisfied by fellatio, I naturally do not know whether you are willing to do this sexual practice.

If two partners react differently to the stimulation of the erogenous zones or are stimulated differently, this makes it more difficult for both partners to trigger an orgasm.

For example, if the man is stimulated very strongly, he can reach orgasm very quickly. Since the arousal curve rises more slouly in woman than in man, it is still below the orgasm threshold at this point. The longer the mutual stimulation of the erogenous zones lasts, the greater the chance that the arousal curves of both partners will exceed the orgasm threshold and that both partners will experience orgasm.

On the basis of this theory I will now explain why you never experienced orgasm during conjugal intercourse. You wrote to me on 7 June that your husband always climaxed after a very short foreplay. At that time your *arousal curve was still far below the orgasm threshold due to the short foreplay. Your husband could certainly not recognize this, because you faked an orgasm for him every time by moaning loudly.*

Because of your religious upbringing, you were also not willing to give yourself an orgasm by hand after your husband's orgasm. Therefore, in 40 years of marriage you have never experienced an orgasm during sexual intercourse.

In conclusion, I will explain why you have an orgasm during sexual intercourse with your current partner. As you could read in the letter you found, I advised your partner to extend foreplay for as long as possible so that your slouly rising arousal curve can exceed the orgasm threshold. Obviously your partner is following this advice exactly. By stimulating your erogenous zones over a long period of time, your arousal curve rises above the orgasm threshold. This is why you experience an orgasm every time you performe a 'duet of lust'.

Yours sincerely

Eros Paradise

Ninth letter

My love,

since we are separated for four days because of the Vienna trip, which I won in the competition, I take the opportunity to thank you once in written form for everything I was able to experience with you. Here in the capital of music, I am thinking above all of the beautiful sonatas that we love to play together passionately during the day, but at nights we love to play them with passion.

Since we enjoyed last year's Christmas concert at the Opera very much, I would ask you to reserve tickets for this year's Christmas concert as soon as possible.

I was very happy about the piano piece 'invitation to dance' which you played on my 90th birthday.

When I found the sexy underwear in your birthday parcel that evening, I was quite perplexed by this 'invitation to have sex'.

Because of my old age, I asked my family doctor the next day if my high blood pressure was a reason not to have sex. When he denied this and gave me the green light to have sex *with the red sexy underwear, I went home immediately to try on the sexy underwear. Fortunately you had bought the right cup size. After I had put on the push-up bra, I looked at myself in the mirror. What luck! The bra fit perfectly.*

Due to the dexterity of my fingers, which I owe to playing the violin, you react surprisingly strongly to the stimulation of your erogenous zones. This is why I was able to write in my diary on August 1ˢᵗ:

'Yesterday my sweetheart had the first orgasm without sexy underwear. In the future our 'duet of lust' will sound in the dark and I can climax by the long awaited stimulation of my breasts.'

In the course of marital compulsory intercourse my orgasm never lasted longer than my husband's orgasm, so only a few seconds. But you, my love, bring me to multiple orgasms lasting several minutes each time. After our last 'duet of lust', the noble lady, who has been living on the ground floor of our villa since August, said something indignant:

"Tonight I woke up with your loud moan. At the age of 80, can't you moan a little softer?"

This sentence suddenly made me realize:

37

*Due to the **fountain of youth** of our 'duets of lust' I now look 10 years younger.*

(I take the liberty of interrupting the letter for a comment: A study carried out by the Royal Edinburgh Hospital on 3500 participants aged 18 to 102 found that an active love life is a major contributor to looking younger.)

How good sex is for the health, I unfortunately did not discover until I was 90 years old. Before we met I often had infectious diseases. This has not been the case for a year now.

(Allow me, dear readers, to interrupt the letter and give you a medical explanation: With age the immune system of the body becomes weaker. That is why people over 60 years of age should definitely take part in the annual flu vaccination, because the vaccine generates specific antibodies against certain flu viruses. However, there is also a very pleasant method to increase the general immune system's resistance: regular sexual activity.

This was proven by the following study conducted by the Swiss Federal Institute of Technology in Zurich:

In men, the number of 'killer cells' in the blood before and after an orgasm triggered by masturbation was determined. The surprising result was that the number of 'killer cells' doubled after the orgasm.'Killer cells' are the immune system's main weapon against pathogens that invade the body. They recognise cells that are infected with pathogens and kill them. Another study found:

Sex once or twice a week leads to a 30 percent increase in the antibody immunoglobulin A. This antibody kills virus-infected cells on mucous membranes.

The **fountain of health** of sexual activities therefore helps the immune system to fight off pathogens and thus makes an important contribution to protection against infectious diseases.

I also cope with stress situations much better than before.

(Allow me, dear readers, to add a comment to this experience of Miss Eve: In a scientific study, women were exposed to a standardized stress dose. The women in the first study group who had previously received an erotic massage from their partners, released smaller amounts of the stress hormone 'cortisol' than the women in the comparison group who had not previously been massaged. The **fountain of health** of sexual activities therefore protects against harmful stress.

Before we met I often had problems falling asleep and sleeping through the night. After our 'duet of lust' I sink into a deep sleep every time and only wake up in the morning. I found an explanation for the refreshing, healthy sleep in a women's magazine:

An American study with 1800 participants found that during orgasm brain is flooded with the hormone 'oxytocin', which has a soporific effect.

*Due to the **fountain of health** of our 'duets of lust', the age-related fat pads have fortunately receded in you and me. I read in the same magazine: A study by the Canadian University of Quebec found that during one our of sex, men burn 100 calories and women 70.*

My migraine pains have improved significantly as a result of our regular sexual activities. I read in the same magazine:

The hormone 'endorphin' released during sex has a similar chemical structure to 'morphine' and therefore relieves menstrual cramps and migraine pain. Hopefully this article has not been read by men. Otherwise, if we women do not feel like having sex, we will no longer be able to refuse to have it by referring to our migraines.

An 80 years old girlfriend of mine said to me the other day:

"After orgasm me and my partner get depressed every time we have an orgasm."

For this case I also had a tip from my women's magazine ready, which I passed on to my girlfriend:

"Sexual arousal below the orgasm threshold also causes the release of the happiness hormone 'dopamine'. You should therefore restrict yourself to stimulating erogenous zones below the orgasm threshold."

On her 100th birthday my mother said:

"Never in my life have I felt as good as I do today."

I, too, am feeling better than ever before in my 91st year, because you give me a second spring in the autumn of my life.

*Our 70-year old single lodger takes 15 tablets per day for all kinds age-related complaints. I don't need a single tablet. Due to the **fountain of health** of our 'duets of lust' my high blood pressure has normalized. That's why I was able to stop taking the antihypertensive tablets.*

Since your parents also lived to be over 100 years old and since there is a formula in medicine that can be used to calculate one's own life expectancy based on the lifetime of father and mother, there is a great chance that we will also be able to celebrate our 100th birthday together. There is a second reason for this. In a study by British scientists I read:

41

Because of the **fountain of youth** of sexual activity, sexually active people have a considerably higher life expectancy than people who abstain.

A survey of 15-year-old girls showed that the most sexually active group (37 %) has already sexual intercourse. The average life expectancy of women is 83 years and the average frequency of sexual intercourse is two times a week. The most sexually active group of women therefore has sexual intercourse about 7000 times. About 10 percent of women reach orgasm during each sexual intercourse. It can therefore be said with certainty: The most sexually active group of women experience an average of 700 orgasms during sexual intercourse in the course of their lives.

Our 'duet of lust' also sounds twice a week. This way we experience an orgasm every time. While the most sexually active group of women experience 700 orgasms during sexual intercourse in the course of 68 years, on my 100th birthday I will gratefully remember approximately 1000 orgasms I was allowed to experience with you in the course of only ten years.

Half a year before my 90th birthday I published two newspaper advertisements. You know the text of the first *advertisement, as our love story began with this advertisement. The following text of the second advertisement you do not know:*

Lady in her 90th year, without heirs, wishes to bequeath her villa in her will in exchange for the payment of a monthly life annuity of 10 000 euros.

While I received many replies to the first advertisement because I had concealed my old age, the information about my old age in the second advertisement motivated many estate agents to reply. They speculated that they would be able to purchase the villa at a favourable price through the foreseeable death of the owner and than make a large profit by selling it.

In order to secure my life annuity in the long term, I stipulated in the contract that the annuity payment obligation would be transferred to the children in the event of the death of my contract partner and concluded the contract with a broker who has 5 children. Due to the fountain of youth of our 'duets of lust', there is a high probability that my contractual partner will ultimately be the loser and I the winner.

On 24 July, I withdrew 20 000 Euros from my life annuity account at the bank and deposed the notes in the piano, a completely safe hiding place. Yesterday my bank informed me by e-mail about the total amount of life annuity payments received up to now: 120 000 euros.

When we celebrate my 100th birthday, the amount of paid life annuities will be 1 200 000 euros. Since the value of my villa was estimated by an expert at 400 000 euros, I have not only experienced 1000 orgasms with you in the period of 10 years, but also won the handsome profit of 800 000 euros.

I am glad that thanks to this life annuity I always have a well-filled travel budget for us.

Today I found a catalogue here in the hotel, in which the most luxurious wellness hotels of the world, scattered over several continents, were presented. After looking trough the catalogue, I suddenly had an idea how I could thank you and at the same time promote our joint project for the future: to celebrate the 100th birthday in the best of health due to the fountain of youth of our 'duets of lust'.

Next spring we are going on a world tour together. During this trip we will be pampered and beautified in the best wellness hotels. Your birthday we will celebrate in San Francisco, mine in Singapore. On this trip we will no longer walk along the Rhine but long the banks of the Mississippi, Amazon, Nile and Yangtze River. The motto of this trip is:

'Around the world in 90 days at the age of 90 years.'

100 kisses

your sweetheart

From the same author

Constance Wolfgang	The best method for success on the stock market
Constance Wolfgang	Italian in 10 days
Constance Wolfgang	French in 10 days